Landlords and Tenants Against Evictions

Housing Justice in Action

Dan Paul

ProAct 2525

Introduction

Introduction to: *Landlords and Tenants Against Evictions*

The government evicts millions of people each year, leaving a trail of devastation in its wake. Families are torn apart, individuals are thrust into homelessness or forced to live in overcrowded and often dangerous conditions with friends or relatives, and entire communities suffer. This eviction crisis is not just a disaster for tenants but also for many landlords, who find themselves embroiled in a system that drains their time, energy, and resources. Paradoxically, the mechanism designed to resolve housing disputes—evictions—exacerbates the problems it aims to address.

The eviction crisis raises a critical question: why are landlords and tenants, often perceived as adversaries, united in their opposition to this process? The answer lies in the shared burdens and inefficiencies of a broken housing system. Evictions drive up the cost of housing, create legal entanglements, and result in significant financial losses for both parties. It is time for a collective reimagining of housing solutions that prioritize stability, affordability, and collaboration over conflict.

The Costs of Evictions

Evictions are not a zero-sum game where one party gains while the other loses. Instead, they are a lose-lose scenario for nearly everyone involved. Tenants lose their homes and endure the trauma, financial strain, and instability that come with being displaced. On the other hand, landlords are saddled with legal fees, lost rental income, and the challenges of re-renting properties in a strained housing market. Beyond the immediate financial costs, evictions create long-term economic and social consequences for communities as a whole.

Why Landlords Are Against Evictions

1 Avoiding Lawsuits: Landlords do not want to engage in costly and time-consuming lawsuits. Legal battles drain resources that could be better spent maintaining properties or addressing tenants' needs.

2 Financial Losses: Evictions often leave landlords with unpaid rent, legal fees, and the expense of repairing and re-renting their properties. In many cases, eviction costs far outweigh the potential benefits.

3 Increased Housing Costs: The eviction process drives up the overall cost of housing. Higher costs mean tenants struggle to pay rent, perpetuating a cycle that harms both landlords and tenants.

4 Time and Energy: Landlords are forced to devote substantial time and energy to navigating a convoluted eviction system, detracting from their ability to manage their properties effectively.

Why Tenants Are Against Evictions

1 Housing, Not Lawsuits: Tenants want a safe and stable place to live, not the upheaval of a lawsuit or eviction process.

2 Trauma and Instability: Evictions are profoundly traumatizing. Being uprooted from one's home disrupts lives, causes emotional distress, and often leads to economic hardship.

3 Wastefulness: Evictions waste resources that could be used to address the root causes of housing instability, such as job loss or unexpected medical expenses.

The Government's Role in the Eviction Crisis

If both landlords and tenants are harmed by evictions, why does the system persist? The answer lies in systemic failures and misplaced priorities.

1 Failure to Provide Housing: The government has not fulfilled its responsibility to ensure housing for all. Private enterprises, driven by profit motives, lack the incentive to build enough affordable housing to meet demand. As a result, millions of people are left without viable housing options.

2 Protecting Profits Over People: Housing policies often prioritize the interests of investors and developers over those of tenants and landlords. This profit-driven approach exacerbates inequality and housing insecurity.

3 Economic Shortcomings: The economy fails to produce enough jobs that pay living wages, making it increasingly difficult for people to afford rent or qualify for housing. Many individuals are trapped in a system that sets them up to fail, with strict requirements for renting or owning homes that are out of reach for those most in need.

4 Systemic Damage: The housing system itself damages many individuals, leaving them unable to function within its rigid constraints. Evictions are both a symptom and a cause of this systemic failure.

A New Vision for Housing Solutions

This book argues that the current eviction system causes more harm than good. People want housing, not lawsuits or displacement. It is time to shift our priorities and rethink how housing is provided and maintained.

Proposed Reforms

1 Shared Responsibility During Evictions: If the government insists on evictions, it should bear part of the financial burden. During the eviction process, the government should cover 50% of the rent, with tenants responsible for the other half. This would reduce the financial strain on landlords while providing tenants with a pathway to stability.

2 Increased Government Involvement in Housing: The government must step up to provide housing for those who cannot secure it through private means. Private enterprise has shown that it cannot or will not meet the demand for affordable housing. A large-scale investment in low-cost housing would act as a buffer against profiteering and ensure that more people have access to safe and stable homes.

3 Flexible Housing Standards: Many governments enforce housing standards so stringent that livable units remain vacant. Policies should be adjusted to allow tenants to occupy these units while receiving rent deductions for any necessary improvements. This approach would maximize housing availability while empowering tenants to take an active role in maintaining their homes.

4 Affordable Maintenance Models: Housing maintenance should be treated as a public good, with services like plumbing, electrical work, and general repairs made more accessible and affordable. Just as communities benefit from having doctors readily available, they should also have access to maintenance professionals who can ensure that housing remains safe and habitable.

5 Reinforce Existing Structures: Building new housing is expensive and time-consuming. Governments should focus on reinforcing and upgrading existing buildings to withstand challenges such as natural disasters.

The Cost of Inaction

Whether or not the government takes action to address the housing crisis, the public will continue to bear the cost. When people are evicted and left without stable housing, they are more likely to rely on emergency rooms, social services, and even the criminal justice system. Taxpayers and society as a whole bear these costs. By investing in stable housing solutions, we can reduce the need for these services and create healthier, more resilient communities.

Conclusion

Evictions harm everyone involved. Tenants lose their homes and stability, landlords lose money and time, and communities are left to deal with the fallout. The current system is unsustainable, inefficient, and deeply unjust.

Landlords Against Evictions offers a new vision for housing solutions that prioritize stability, collaboration, and equity. By rethinking the role of government, adjusting policies to reflect the realities of the housing market, and fostering partnerships between landlords and tenants, we can build a system that works for everyone. It is time to move beyond evictions and toward a future where housing is a right, not a privilege.

Chapter 1

The Cost of Inaction – Why Housing Must Be a Government Priority

In every corner of the world, governments are facing an urgent dilemma: how to ensure that their citizens have access to safe, stable housing in a rapidly changing world. The question is no longer whether housing should be a priority—it is whether we, as a society, can afford to ignore the dire need for government intervention in housing. The stakes have never been higher.

This is not just a financial issue; it is a human issue. The availability of housing touches every facet of life —security, health, education, social stability, and economic opportunity. Yet, as we enter an era of environmental chaos driven by global warming, the role of governments in securing housing becomes more critical than ever. Housing is not merely a commodity—it is a lifeline, and if governments fail to ensure access to it, the costs will be devastating. The long-term consequences of ignoring this need will far outweigh any immediate savings or political convenience.

In the past, housing was often treated as a market-driven commodity, where supply and demand determined who could afford a place to live. But as the world faces mounting environmental and economic pressures, this model is no longer sustainable. The cost of leaving housing entirely to the private sector is already apparent. Global warming is intensifying, making many areas uninhabitable, and driving up the costs of maintaining existing infrastructure. The housing crisis is no longer affecting only the most vulnerable—it is a ticking time bomb for everyone.

In this first chapter, we will explore why governments must take responsibility for ensuring that all citizens have access to housing. We will examine the economic and social costs of inaction, the dangers posed by climate change, and why a more active, interventionist approach is needed now to avoid even greater catastrophes in the future.

The Changing Landscape: Global Warming and Its Impact on Housing

As the global climate continues to destabilize, it is becoming increasingly clear that many conditions that once made housing accessible and affordable are no longer viable. We are witnessing the beginning of a housing crisis unlike any seen before. The challenges posed by global warming, such as **increased storm frequency**, **wildfires**, **flooding**, and **rising sea levels**, threaten to wipe out entire neighborhoods and force entire populations to flee. In areas where homes once stood proud and strong, the forces of nature now have the upper hand, creating a growing sense of unease among homeowners and renters alike.

Consider, for example, coastal communities. Many cities and towns along the coasts were once thriving hubs of commerce and living, but now, they are rapidly becoming areas at risk of being submerged by rising sea levels. Some areas are already facing **increased flooding**, which makes daily life more dangerous and unpredictable. As the frequency and intensity of storms grow, properties are being destroyed at a higher rate. Families who once lived peacefully in these areas now face the painful prospect of relocation as their homes become unsalvageable.

But this problem isn't limited to coastal areas alone. **Wildfires** in places like California and Australia are burning entire neighborhoods to the ground, leaving families displaced and insurance companies unable to cover the massive damage. **Heatwaves** and **droughts** are driving agricultural failure, which further increases food prices and deepens economic insecurity. People who once lived in these regions may find themselves unable to afford insurance, unable to sell their properties, or unable to find another place to live because climate change has made more areas less habitable.

As these effects unfold, housing is being destroyed at an alarming rate. The homes we once took for granted are increasingly vulnerable to environmental catastrophes, and the social safety nets that should be in place to support those displaced are often woefully insufficient.

The Escalating Costs of Housing Destruction

It's easy to think of housing as a private issue, one that individuals or businesses can manage on their own. But when housing is threatened on a broad scale, the costs of inaction become impossible to ignore. Housing is not just a place to live—it is the foundation of economic stability, social mobility, and personal security. When homes are destroyed by climate-related events, the costs to governments and society are far-reaching and long-lasting.

Consider the escalating costs associated with the aftermath of natural disasters. Governments are often left footing the bill for rebuilding efforts, whether repairing roads, replacing damaged infrastructure, or providing financial assistance to displaced residents. These costs can spiral into the billions of dollars, draining public coffers and diverting resources from other important areas. If the government fails to ensure that communities are prepared for these disasters, those costs will only increase as the impacts of global warming worsen.

In addition to the direct costs of rebuilding, there are long-term economic repercussions. When large areas are rendered uninhabitable, economic activity grinds to a halt. Businesses close, jobs are lost, and workers are forced to relocate to areas that may already be overcrowded. This increases demand for housing, driving up prices even further in strained markets. The economic disruption caused by widespread housing destruction is felt across the entire nation, exacerbating inequality and social unrest.

However, the most dangerous cost of all is the social instability that follows the collapse of housing markets. When entire neighborhoods are wiped out, and thousands of people are displaced, the fabric of society is torn apart. People lose their sense of security, their community ties, and in many cases, their livelihoods. This creates an atmosphere of fear and uncertainty, which can fuel political instability, social conflict, and even mass migration.

The Role of Government: Ensuring Housing Security

Given the profound social, economic, and environmental costs of inaction, the government's role in ensuring housing stability and security is clearer than ever. Governments must recognize that housing is not a luxury—it is a fundamental right. The costs of failing to act will far outweigh the costs of intervention. To avoid future housing crises, governments must take immediate, bold steps to ensure that housing remains accessible, affordable, and resilient in the face of global warming.

1 Investing in Resilient Housing

2 First and foremost, governments must prioritize constructing and retrofitting **resilient housing**. This means investing in buildings that can withstand extreme weather events like high winds, floods, and wildfires. Homes should be built with fire- and flood-resistant materials and able to endure long-term exposure to heatwaves. Homes should be elevated or constructed on higher ground in areas prone to flooding. In wildfire-prone regions, creating defensible space around homes, using non-flammable materials, and installing fire-resistant roofing can make the difference between life and death.

3 Retrofitting existing housing to meet modern climate resilience standards is equally important. Governments can offer **subsidies** and **incentives** for homeowners to make these improvements, ensuring that existing homes are not left vulnerable to climate-related damage.

4 Upgrading Infrastructure

5 Beyond individual homes, governments must focus on upgrading **infrastructure** to support resilient housing. Roads, utilities, and communications systems should be built or retrofitted to withstand extreme weather events. This includes things like

flood defenses, storm-resistant power grids, and **renewable energy sources** that are less susceptible to disruption. Ensuring that cities are equipped with resilient infrastructure is essential to both protecting homes and providing a foundation for future development.

6 Affordable Housing and Government Support

7 The housing crisis exacerbated by global warming is not just a matter of building stronger homes—it's also about **ensuring that housing remains affordable and accessible** to all people. Governments must step in to provide subsidies for those in need, including renters, low-income homeowners, and communities displaced by climate disasters. Additionally, governments should provide **low-interest loans** and grants to help people rebuild after disasters. This ensures that those with the greatest need are not left behind in the scramble for shelter.

8 Insurance and Financial Protection

9 The collapse of insurance markets in high-risk areas is one of the greatest threats to housing stability in a warming world. To address this, governments must intervene to provide **affordable insurance** options for homeowners in high-risk areas. Governments can create **re-insurance schemes** that help stabilize the insurance market and prevent massive premium increases. Ensuring that people have access to affordable insurance helps protect

their homes and prevents families from falling into poverty after a disaster.

10 Managed Retreat and Relocation Support

11 A managed retreat may be necessary in areas where it is no longer feasible or safe to live. Governments should invest in **relocation programs** that assist people in moving away from high-risk areas. This involves providing financial support to those who need to relocate and helping them find new, safe places to live. Relocation programs also need to focus on creating **new, sustainable housing in safer areas**, ensuring that displaced populations are not left without the means to rebuild their lives.

Conclusion: The Urgency of Action

The reality is that without government intervention, the cost of inaction on housing will be much greater than the status quo. As global warming continues to wreak havoc on the environment, the toll on housing will only increase. Governments must recognize that investing in housing is not just an act of charity—it is an act of self-preservation.

If governments fail to step up, they will face higher costs in the long term, both in terms of financial losses and social instability. Housing is not a luxury or a market-driven commodity; it is a fundamental right, and it is time for governments to fulfill their duty to ensure that every person has a safe place to live. The cost of doing nothing is simply too high.

Chapter 2

The True Cost of Evictions - How the Government's Eviction Program Damages Landlords, Tenants, and Society at Large

Evictions are often framed as a simple, necessary legal process—a tool for landlords to reclaim their properties when tenants fail to pay rent or violate lease terms. On the surface, the eviction process might seem like a way to protect property rights and maintain the stability of rental markets. However, when viewed from a broader perspective, evictions reveal themselves to be a deeply damaging practice for all parties involved: landlords, tenants, and society as a whole. The costs of eviction are far greater than most people realize, and the government's role in enforcing evictions has only exacerbated the problem.

This chapter will examine the true economic and social costs of eviction, focusing on how both tenants and landlords suffer in the aftermath of these proceedings. We will look at the ways in which the government's eviction program—designed to protect landlords and ensure the smooth functioning of rental markets—ultimately causes more harm than good. From increasing housing instability to raising costs for everyone, the current eviction system has far-reaching consequences that could be avoided if the government focused on more effective housing solutions.

The Eviction Process: A Legal Mechanism with High Hidden Costs

In most cases, eviction begins when a tenant fails to pay rent or violates the terms of their lease agreement. In many cities, the eviction process can take months to complete, requiring landlords to navigate complex legal frameworks, court systems, and enforcement agencies. While eviction laws aim to protect property owners' rights, the results often backfire, creating a cascade of negative consequences for tenants and landlords.

The Cost to Tenants: Displacement and Economic Hardship

For tenants, the consequences of eviction can be devastating. Losing one's home is traumatic and disruptive, leading to a range of social, psychological, and economic problems. One of the most significant consequences of eviction is the immediate financial hardship it creates. Most people who are evicted are already struggling financially, and eviction is often the final blow that pushes them further into poverty.

1 Financial Burden: The costs of eviction for tenants are enormous. According to the *Eviction Lab* at Princeton University, approximately **2.7 million eviction filings** occur in the United States every year, and an estimated **900,000 households** are forcibly evicted. Evictions are not only expensive for tenants in terms of lost deposits, moving costs, and finding new housing, but they also have lasting financial consequences. Evicted tenants often face **higher rent costs** in future housing due to a poor rental history, and they are frequently required to pay **upfront deposits** and application fees for new places. For many, finding new housing after an eviction becomes an almost impossible task due to the stigma of eviction on their rental history.

2 Housing Instability and Homelessness: According to the *National Low-Income Housing Coalition* (NLIHC), the **lack of affordable housing** in the U.S. is one of the leading causes of eviction. As rents increase, particularly in major urban centers, more and more people are being forced out of their homes. These individuals often find themselves in a precarious housing situation, with nowhere to go and no viable housing options available. The number of **homeless people** in the U.S. has risen sharply over the last decade, with approximately **650,000 people** homeless on any given night as of 2024. Many of these individuals were likely evicted from their homes, with nowhere to go afterward.

3 Psychological and Social Damage: The trauma of eviction extends beyond financial hardship. Tenants who are evicted frequently suffer from **anxiety, depression, and emotional distress**. Losing one's home and facing uncertainty about the future can cause severe psychological damage, particularly for children and families. Research from the *American Psychological Association* has shown that families who experience eviction are more likely to experience **disruptions in their children's education, health, and well-being**. The social isolation and stigma associated with eviction further deepen the sense of despair and helplessness.

The Cost to Landlords: Unintended Consequences and Financial Losses

While landlords are often seen as the "victims" in eviction proceedings, the financial and logistical costs of evictions are considerable, and many landlords end up suffering just as much—if not more—than their tenants.

1 Lost Rent and Legal Costs: The financial burden of eviction for landlords is significant. First, landlords lose **months of rent** while the eviction process plays out, often leaving them with little recourse to recoup these losses. While tenants are evicted for non-payment, the landlord must cover their own costs for utilities, property maintenance, and legal fees. These expenses often add up to **thousands of dollars** before the eviction is finalized.

2 For example, one study by the *Urban Institute* found that the average cost to a landlord for an eviction—including legal fees, lost rent, and administrative expenses—can reach between **$3,500 and $5,500 per eviction**. This is a significant loss for small-scale landlords, who rely on steady rental income to cover property maintenance and mortgages.

3 Property Damage: In many eviction cases, tenants leave behind significant **damage to the property**, from broken windows to holes in walls or carpets. While landlords can seek to recoup some of these damages through the security deposit, it's often insufficient to cover the full cost of repairs. Furthermore, if the tenant has skipped out without paying rent or causing damage, the landlord may be unable to recover any of their losses.

4 Vacancy Loss: Once a tenant has been evicted, the property often remains **vacant** for extended periods. Finding a new tenant can take weeks or even months, during which the landlord earns no rental income. Additionally, landlords often face additional expenses while trying to advertise the unit, repair damages, or clean the property.

5 Legal and Administrative Costs: The eviction process itself is also costly for landlords in terms of **legal fees**. In many states, landlords are required to go through a formal legal process, involving court hearings and the services of an attorney. The costs of filing for eviction and obtaining a judgment can quickly add up, further squeezing landlords' margins.

The Societal Cost: Housing Instability, Crime, and Increased Public Spending

While the immediate costs to tenants and landlords are significant, the broader societal impact of evictions is even more damaging. The housing crisis is a public health and economic crisis, and evictions play a central role in exacerbating these problems.

1 Increased Homelessness: As mentioned earlier, evictions are a leading cause of **homelessness**, which has been steadily rising in the United States. Homelessness places a tremendous strain on local governments, healthcare systems, and social services. Homeless individuals often rely on emergency shelters, food programs, and healthcare services, which are costly for the government to provide. According to a report by the *National Alliance to End Homelessness*, the **annual cost of homelessness** in the U.S. is estimated to be **$12 billion**. Much of this cost comes from the **healthcare** and **social services** required to manage the homeless population, which could be avoided by preventing eviction in the first place.

2 Crime and Social Instability: Research has also shown that people who experience eviction are more likely to become involved in **criminal activity**. The disruption caused by eviction can lead to **substance abuse, mental health issues**, and increased involvement with the criminal justice system. For example, a study by the *Urban Institute* found that people who were evicted from their homes were **twice as likely** to be arrested as those who remained housed. The societal cost of this involvement with the criminal justice system—both in terms of policing and incarceration—is staggering.

3 Decreased Economic Productivity: When people lose their homes, they often lose their jobs. The **disruption caused by eviction**—having to move, finding new housing, and coping with the emotional toll—makes it harder for tenants to stay employed or maintain steady income. The *Economic Policy Institute* has estimated that the cost of **housing instability** to the broader economy—through reduced productivity, increased healthcare costs, and the strain on public services—is approximately **$3.3 billion per year**.

The Economic Damage of Evictions: What Could We Do With That Money?

The financial cost of eviction to both tenants and landlords is significant, but it is nothing compared to the larger economic and societal toll that evictions take. However, what if the money spent on evictions—on court costs, lost rent, legal fees, healthcare expenses, and social services—was instead redirected toward solutions that provide housing for the people who need it most?

Instead of pouring resources into a broken system that does more harm than good, governments could invest that money into **affordable housing initiatives**, rental assistance programs, and **housing-first policies** that prioritize stable housing as a solution to homelessness. If we redirected even a fraction of the costs associated with evictions into programs that help people **rent or own** their homes, the long-term savings could be astronomical.

1 Affordable Housing: For example, if governments used funds currently spent on eviction-related costs to invest in the construction of **affordable housing**, the supply of affordable units would increase, making it easier for low-income individuals to find stable housing. According to the *National Low-Income Housing Coalition*, the U.S. is currently facing a **deficit of 7 million affordable rental homes** for extremely low-income renters. By addressing this shortage, we could significantly reduce eviction rates, alleviate homelessness, and stabilize rental markets.

2 Rental Assistance Programs: Rental assistance programs, such as **Section 8 Housing Vouchers**, have been proven to help low-income tenants maintain housing stability. The government could increase funding for these programs, allowing more individuals and families to afford rent without falling behind and facing eviction.

3 Housing-First Initiatives: Housing-first programs, which focus on providing stable housing without preconditions such as sobriety or employment, have been shown to be highly effective in reducing homelessness and improving the health and well-being of participants. By funding these programs, governments could address the root causes of eviction—lack of affordable housing—while also providing much-needed support to vulnerable populations.

Conclusion: Time for a Paradigm Shift

Evictions are a costly, inefficient, and harmful practice for tenants, landlords, and society at large. The government's eviction program, while intended to maintain stability in the rental market, ultimately does more harm than good. The financial, psychological, and social costs are staggering, and they could be avoided by shifting the focus from eviction enforcement to more effective housing solutions.

By investing in affordable housing, rental assistance programs, and housing-first initiatives, governments could reduce eviction rates, improve housing stability, and lower the long-term costs to society. The current system is broken, and it's time for a paradigm shift. Rather than perpetuating a system that causes widespread harm, we must focus on creating a society where housing is a right, not a privilege.

Chapter 3

The Problem with Mansions and Wasteful Housing – Redefining Living Space for a Sustainable Future

The way we live is changing. Over the past century, housing in developed countries has increasingly become a symbol of excess, a visual manifestation of wealth, and a signifier of success. In the process, we have moved far away from the notion of housing as shelter—simple, functional, and efficient—and instead embraced an image of housing as a status symbol, a display of grandeur and affluence.

Among the clearest representations of this trend are **mansions**, those sprawling, over-sized homes that often stretch well beyond the average person's need for shelter. Today, it's not uncommon to see homes that span **5,000 square feet**, **10,000 square feet**, or even larger. These homes are designed to accommodate more than just a family's basic needs—they are designed to impress, dominate, and serve as monuments to wealth. But what are we really gaining from these massive living spaces, and what are we sacrificing in terms of environmental sustainability, economic efficiency, and social equity?

In this chapter, we will critique the cultural and environmental cost of housing that exceeds **500 square feet per person**, with particular emphasis on the ecological and social consequences of **mansions**. We will explore the **waste in construction**, the **inefficiencies** of oversized homes, and how the government can change building codes to shift the focus toward more sustainable, equitable, and modest housing.

The Cultural Fascination with Mansions

Mansions are not merely homes; they are symbols of success. In many ways, owning a mansion is equated with achieving the pinnacle of the American Dream—the notion that, through hard work and perseverance, one can attain limitless wealth and social status. A mansion often signals a life of comfort, luxury, and opulence. It is meant to be more than a place of shelter; it is a place of display, where living rooms are designed for entertainment rather than basic habitation, and guest bathrooms rival the size of entire apartments.

But beyond the aesthetics, what exactly does a mansion offer that a smaller, more functional home cannot? The reality is that many features commonly found in mansions—such as multiple guest rooms, expansive kitchens, and luxury amenities like home theaters and indoor pools—serve no practical purpose beyond indulgence. These homes offer space for activities that most people rarely engage in or need.

In fact, when you examine the average home size in the U.S., it becomes clear that homes have been growing exponentially over the last few decades. According to the *U.S. Census Bureau*, the average size of a new single-family home in 1950 was around **983 square feet**. By 2020, this had ballooned to more than **2,500 square feet**. Homes designed for families of four or fewer are now being built with the square footage to accommodate much larger families, even though these large families rarely exist anymore. In contrast, people today often opt for smaller households, yet their homes are growing larger. This disconnect between the number of people living in these homes and the size of the homes themselves is a testament to how our priorities have shifted toward excess.

While homes have grown larger, **global population growth**, **diminishing resources**, and rising environmental crises have raised fundamental questions about how we should think about space and consumption. When we examine the ecological footprint of these massive homes, the argument against mansions becomes clear.

The Environmental Impact of Mansions and Wasteful Housing

Larger homes are, by their very nature, more resource-intensive. They consume far more **materials** in construction, **energy** for heating and cooling, and **water** for plumbing. This excessive consumption has significant consequences for the environment and society.

1 Material Waste: Building a mansion requires an enormous amount of materials—bricks, cement, steel, wood, glass, insulation, and more. While these materials are necessary for construction, the sheer scale of what is consumed in building mansions is staggering. According to the *Environmental Protection Agency* (EPA), the construction industry is responsible for about **40% of the world's energy-related carbon emissions** and **35% of global material use**. With their sprawling square footage and elaborate designs, Mansions are among the primary contributors to this environmental burden.

2 Building homes larger than 500 square feet per person increases the demand for raw materials and contributes to a higher **carbon footprint** due to transportation, energy use, and waste. Building a single large home can consume as much energy and resources as several smaller homes would require. **Construction waste**—from leftover materials to discarded debris—also adds to the environmental toll. In the U.S. alone, the construction industry generates more than **160 million tons of waste** annually, much of it from residential construction.

3 Energy Consumption: The energy consumption of mansions is disproportionately high compared to smaller homes. Heating and cooling large spaces require significantly more energy than maintaining a smaller, more efficient home. Even when homes are equipped with energy-efficient appliances, the sheer size of the home means more energy is required to maintain comfortable living conditions.

4 In fact, a 5,000-square-foot mansion might require more energy to operate than several smaller homes combined. According to the *U.S. Department of Energy*, the average home in the U.S. consumes about **10,649 kilowatt-hours of electricity per year**. A mansion, with its additional square footage, may easily exceed **20,000 kilowatt-hours** annually, particularly if it includes expansive common areas, multiple bathrooms, and luxury features like heated floors or a large pool.

5 The environmental impact of this energy usage cannot be understated. Even as renewable energy sources like solar and wind become more mainstream, the fact remains that **overconsumption** of energy is unsustainable. With rising global temperatures and increasing demand for power, reducing overall energy consumption is critical to minimizing climate change. Reducing the size of homes—particularly those that go beyond 500 square feet per person—could go a long way toward cutting the energy demands of the residential sector.

6 **Water Use**: Along with energy, the construction and operation of mansions also demand large quantities of **water**. This includes water for construction processes as well as water used in daily activities, such as in pools, fountains, and irrigation systems. Many mansions are equipped with extensive **landscaping**, which may include manicured lawns, gardens, and water features—further increasing their water consumption. These water-intensive amenities waste vital resources, especially in areas already experiencing water shortages.

7 In California, for example, **outdoor water usage** accounts for nearly **50%** of residential water consumption. Larger homes with sprawling lawns and gardens exacerbate this problem. The excessive water use that accompanies mansion living—often seen as a symbol of luxury—is not only wasteful but unsustainable in a world facing growing water scarcity.

The Social Inequities of Mansions

In addition to the environmental and material costs, mansions contribute to **social inequity**. While the owners of these expansive homes enjoy large spaces for leisure and luxury, many people across the globe struggle to meet their basic housing needs. As the gap between the rich and the poor continues to grow, mansions stand as an enduring symbol of this inequality—homes for the few, built on a foundation of

resource exploitation and **environmental degradation**.

The focus on large, opulent homes also exacerbates the **housing crisis**, particularly in urban areas. As developers prioritize constructing luxury homes and mansions to cater to the wealthy, they often ignore the pressing need for **affordable housing**. This leads to **gentrification**, where working-class and low-income families are priced out of neighborhoods, further entrenching social divides.

The number of **homeless individuals** in the U.S. has surged, with **650,000 people** experiencing homelessness on any given night. Many of these individuals would benefit from smaller, affordable homes that prioritize practical living rather than excess. However, while **mansions** continue to be built for a select few, the need for affordable housing for the many is ignored.

Reducing the Size and Waste: How Government Can Change Building Codes

The solution to the problem of oversized homes lies in rethinking our approach to housing and construction. Governments have a critical role to play in **shaping housing policy** and ensuring that homes are built with sustainability, efficiency, and fairness in mind. One of the most effective ways to address the wasteful construction of large homes—particularly those exceeding 500 square feet per person—is by revising **building codes** and **zoning laws** to promote more modest, functional housing.

1 Limiting Square Footage per Person: Governments can impose regulations that restrict the size of homes relative to the number of occupants. While such laws may not require the outright banning of large homes, they could **set limits** on the maximum square footage allowed for each person living in the home. For instance, a policy could mandate that new homes or residential developments should not exceed **500 square feet per person**. This would help prevent the construction of mansions and force developers to focus on building homes that are more in line with the actual needs of their occupants rather than indulging in excess.

2 Encouraging Multi-Use Spaces: Another solution would be to promote the **design of multi-functional spaces** that allow families to live comfortably in smaller homes without sacrificing quality of life. For example, **modular homes** and **tiny houses** can serve as models for efficient, sustainable living. Governments can incentivize the design and construction of these homes by offering tax breaks or subsidies to developers and homeowners.

3 Incentivizing Sustainable Materials and Practices: Building codes could be updated to encourage the use of more **sustainable materials** and **construction practices**. This includes mandating the use of recycled materials, energy-efficient insulation, and green building technologies. Governments could also require that new homes meet specific energy and water efficiency standards, ensuring that they have a smaller environmental footprint than traditional mansions.

4 Revising Zoning Laws to Prioritize Affordability: Zoning laws can be adapted to reduce the incentive for building luxury homes on large plots of land, particularly in urban areas. By setting aside land for **affordable housing developments** and restricting the construction of large, single-family homes, governments can address both housing shortages and environmental concerns. Mixed-use zoning can allow for more efficient land use, with a blend of residential, commercial, and recreational spaces that promote community building and reduce the need for sprawling mansions.

Conclusion

The era of the mansion, with its sprawling square footage and excessive consumption of materials and energy, is a symbol of the inequality, waste, and unsustainable practices that have come to define modern housing. If we are to address the growing housing crisis and mitigate the environmental destruction caused by excessive construction, we must rethink our approach to homebuilding.

Governments have the power to guide this shift through policies limiting the size of homes relative to their occupants, incentivizing sustainable practices, and prioritizing affordable housing creation. By embracing these changes, we can build a future in which housing is a **right**—not a privilege—and where homes serve the practical needs of all people rather than being monuments to excess.

Chapter 4

The Roots of Homelessness and Pathways to Lasting Solutions

Part 1: Who Are the Homeless and Why Are They Homeless?

Homelessness is not a monolithic condition; it encompasses a broad spectrum of people, each with their own stories, backgrounds, and reasons for being without a stable home. At its core, homelessness is the manifestation of systemic failures within society, where economic, social, and political structures fail to meet the needs of some of the most vulnerable people. While the causes of homelessness are complex, they can be broadly understood as a product of structural inequality, individual misfortune, and societal neglect.

A. The Faces of Homelessness

Homelessness includes people from various walks of life, including:

- **Families with children**: Often the most visible form of homelessness in urban areas, families may find themselves living in shelters or on the streets after losing housing due to job loss, medical emergencies, or the unaffordability of rent.

- **Youth and young adults**: Many young people experience homelessness after being kicked out of their homes or aging out of foster care. With limited job prospects and often no family safety net, they find themselves struggling to survive.

- **Individuals with mental illness**: Mental health conditions, particularly untreated or undiagnosed ones, often make it difficult for individuals to maintain steady housing. The lack of supportive services for those with mental health issues exacerbates this problem.

- **Veterans**: Many veterans face homelessness due to a combination of post-traumatic stress disorder (PTSD), substance abuse, and difficulties reintegrating into civilian life. The lack of adequate support systems for veterans further complicates their situation.

- **People with substance abuse disorders**: While substance abuse is not a direct cause of homelessness, the combination of addiction and a lack of supportive housing or treatment can lead people to the streets.

• **Low-wage workers and the working poor**: With rising rents and stagnant wages, many working-class individuals and families find themselves on the brink of homelessness. Even with full-time employment, housing can be unaffordable when wages do not keep pace with the rising cost of living.

B. Why Are People Homeless?

Homelessness is largely driven by a confluence of economic, societal, and personal factors. Some of the primary reasons people become homeless include:

1 The Affordable Housing Crisis: At the heart of the housing crisis is the shortage of affordable homes. Between the growing demand for housing and the inability of wages to keep up with rising housing costs, many families and individuals simply cannot afford a roof over their heads. A combination of rent inflation, rising property values, and gentrification has pushed many people out of their homes and into precarious living situations.

2 Income Inequality: The widening gap between the rich and the poor has resulted in the concentration of wealth in the hands of a few while many working-class families struggle to make ends meet. Income inequality limits access to housing, healthcare, and social services, leaving many vulnerable to homelessness.

3 Lack of Supportive Services: Mental health care, addiction treatment, and social services are often underfunded, and many people who are at risk of homelessness do not have access to the care they need. A lack of affordable mental health services means many individuals with untreated conditions end up on the streets.

4 Evictions and Foreclosures: Evictions have risen in recent years, often linked to increasing rents or changes in landlords' business practices. A single eviction can set off a chain of events that leaves a person or family without stable housing. Foreclosures similarly displace homeowners, and the transition to renting can be financially precarious.

5 Criminal Justice System: The mass incarceration of marginalized communities, particularly Black and Latino individuals, has contributed to homelessness. Many individuals exiting the prison system find it difficult to reintegrate into society, largely due to a lack of housing options, criminal records, and limited access to employment opportunities.

6 Structural Racism: Systemic racism in housing policies—such as redlining, discriminatory lending practices, and unequal access to housing—has disproportionately affected people of color. This legacy of inequality continues to contribute to higher rates of homelessness among African Americans, Latinos, and Native Americans.

C. Society's Role in Creating Homelessness

Homelessness is not simply a result of individual failings or bad luck. It is largely a product of a society that prioritizes profit over people, the individual over the collective, and short-term solutions over long-term structural change. Market-driven housing policies, disinvestment in public housing, cuts to social welfare programs, and the criminalization of homelessness have all contributed to the current crisis.

Rather than providing safety nets and opportunities for economic mobility, society has often responded to homelessness with criminalization, stigmatization, and punitive measures, further entrenching people in cycles of poverty and displacement. The absence of affordable housing and insufficient mental health and addiction treatment services have created a perfect storm in which people are left to fall through the cracks, often with little recourse or support.

Part 2: Solutions to Homelessness: Preparing People to Own, Operate, and Maintain Housing

Addressing homelessness requires a multifaceted approach—one that not only provides immediate relief but also tackles the root causes and supports long-term stability. Solutions must focus on providing housing, increasing access to services, and reforming systems like education, employment, and the criminal justice system. By restructuring key societal institutions, it is possible to create a system that helps people secure housing and empowers them to maintain it.

A. The Role of Institutions in Supporting Housing Security

1 Prisons and the Criminal Justice System: A significant portion of the homeless population has been impacted by the criminal justice system. Reforms that reduce the criminalization of homelessness, end the cycle of incarceration, and provide alternatives to prison—such as restorative justice and community-based corrections—would prevent many from losing their housing and stability in the first place.

o **Reintegration Programs**: For those exiting prison, the government should invest in reintegration programs that provide not only housing but also job training, counseling, and educational opportunities. These programs should be tailored to ensure a successful transition back into society, including affordable housing options.

o **Decriminalization of Homelessness**: Rather than arresting people for being homeless or engaging in minor infractions, society should focus on decriminalizing homelessness. Policies such as "Housing First," which provide immediate access to permanent housing with wraparound services, are far more effective than punitive measures.

2 Schools: Education is a powerful tool in breaking the cycle of poverty and homelessness. Schools must play a larger role in preparing young people for future housing stability by teaching financial literacy, offering career and vocational training, and providing housing assistance for students who experience homelessness.

○ **Housing and Education Integration**: Schools could partner with housing agencies to provide educational support and practical assistance to students at risk of homelessness. This might include connecting students with emergency housing, financial support programs, or even legal advocacy if their families are facing eviction.

○ **Youth Housing Programs**: Young people, particularly those aging out of foster care, need specific support. By creating programs that offer a pathway to stable housing—such as guaranteed rental assistance or shared housing for young adults—society can prevent these individuals from falling into homelessness as they transition to adulthood.

3 Workplaces: A stable income is one of the most significant factors in housing stability. Employers can help by providing more affordable housing options through employer-assisted housing programs, offering higher wages, and ensuring that workers have access to benefits like healthcare and paid leave that can prevent them from losing housing.

o **Living Wage Legislation**: One of the most direct solutions to homelessness is to address wage inequality. Raising the minimum wage to a livable level, adjusting for inflation, and ensuring that housing remains affordable for low-income workers would significantly reduce homelessness.

o **Workplace Housing Benefits**: Employers could offer housing stipends or rental assistance to workers in high-cost areas, or partner with affordable housing developers to create workforce housing near job centers..

4 Community and Social Networks: One of the most effective ways to prevent and alleviate homelessness is through community-based solutions. By encouraging cooperative housing models, co-ownership programs, and multi-generational living, we can create more inclusive housing options that are supportive and affordable.

B. Policy and Legal Changes to Facilitate Housing Access

Several legal and policy changes are necessary to address homelessness effectively. These reforms focus on expanding housing options, ensuring that people can stay housed, and making housing more accessible to all.

1 Zoning Laws: One of the most effective ways to increase the housing supply is by reforming zoning laws. Many cities' zoning laws currently restrict the construction of affordable housing by requiring large minimum lot sizes, banning multi-family housing, and imposing other restrictions that make it difficult to build the housing people need. Reforming these laws to encourage affordable housing development and mixed-use buildings could alleviate housing shortages.

2 **Housing Cooperatives and Shared Living**: To support people who are not part of traditional nuclear families, laws must be changed to allow more flexible living arrangements, such as housing cooperatives, shared living spaces, and communal homes. These models could reduce housing costs and foster a sense of community.

o **Multi-Generational and Non-Familial Housing**: Housing laws should be updated to allow non-family members—such as friends, roommates, or even strangers—to live together legally in the same building or apartment without violating zoning or housing codes. This could involve relaxed regulations around occupancy limits or the creation of incentives for shared housing models.

3 **Rent Control and Tenant Protections**: Rent control laws and tenant protection policies should be expanded to ensure that renters are not unfairly evicted or priced out of their homes. These policies could include rent stabilization measures, longer-term leases, and protections for tenants against discrimination.

4 Universal Rent Subsidies: A nationwide program that guarantees rent subsidies for individuals and families making below a certain income threshold would ensure that people are not priced out of housing markets. This could take the form of direct rental assistance or housing vouchers.

5 Housing First Policies: Finally, Housing First policies should be expanded. These policies prioritize providing individuals with stable, permanent housing first, before addressing any other challenges, such as addiction or mental illness. Providing people with the security of a home is often the first step toward stability and self-sufficiency.

Conclusion

Homelessness is a crisis that has been decades in the making, driven by policies that prioritize profit over people, ignore the needs of the most vulnerable, and fail to address the systemic inequalities that contribute to housing instability. To solve this crisis, society must provide immediate relief and undertake profound changes in how we approach housing, employment, education, and justice. By reforming institutions, enacting supportive policies, and empowering individuals to maintain stable housing, we can create a society where everyone has access to safe, secure, and affordable housing.

Chapter 5

Advancing Solutions for Sustainable Housing: Goals at Local, Regional, and National Levels

Housing is a cornerstone of human well-being, yet achieving sustainable, climate-resilient, and affordable housing remains a challenge. This chapter outlines actionable goals at local, regional, and national levels, emphasizing the use of local materials and labor while leveraging innovation, government initiatives, and community engagement. We also explore how design contests can mobilize stakeholders to catalyze progress.

1. Local-Level Goals: Empowering Communities

At the community level, the focus is on utilizing local resources, minimizing environmental impact, and maximizing community engagement. The goals include:

a. Promoting Local Materials and Labor

Local materials such as bamboo, adobe, or timber are often affordable, sustainable, and culturally appropriate. By engaging local labor, projects stimulate economic growth and build community ownership.

- **Action Plan**:

○ Conduct resource mapping to identify locally available sustainable materials.

○ Train local workers in green construction techniques to ensure high-quality, climate-resilient structures.

b. Strengthening Resilience to Climate Change

Community-level housing must withstand local environmental conditions, including floods, heat waves, and storms.

- **Action Plan**:

○ Design homes with features like raised foundations, natural ventilation, and solar shading.

○ Integrate rainwater harvesting systems and renewable energy sources.

c. Fostering Community Collaboration

Housing initiatives are more effective when local voices are part of the decision-making process.

- **Action Plan**:

○ Establish housing cooperatives or local councils to oversee projects.

○ Hold participatory workshops to co-design solutions with residents.

2. Regional-Level Goals: Coordinating Resources and Policy

At the regional level, efforts should focus on creating a network of sustainable housing initiatives, standardizing practices, and ensuring equitable resource distribution.

a. Regional Housing Hubs

Establish housing hubs to coordinate expertise, funding, and technical resources across municipalities.

- **Action Plan**:

○ Develop centralized networks for sharing best practices and innovations.

○ Offer technical assistance to rural and underserved areas.

b. Policy and Zoning Reform

Zoning laws and building codes must encourage sustainable, low-cost housing solutions.

- **Action Plan**:

○ Revise codes to allow for alternative materials and designs.

○ Incentivize developers with tax breaks for using green methods.

c. Cross-Municipality Collaboration

Regional governments can pool resources and ideas to scale successful models.

- **Action Plan**:

○ Launch inter-city partnerships to replicate successful housing models.

○ Create region-wide goals for affordable housing quotas.

3. National-Level Goals: Scaling Impact and Setting Standards

National governments are critical in setting ambitious targets, providing funding, and fostering innovation.

a. Universal Housing Standards

National policies should set clear, enforceable standards for sustainable housing.

- **Action Plan**:

○ Mandate energy-efficient designs for new construction.

○ Require affordability benchmarks for publicly funded housing projects.

b. Funding and Incentives

Governments can accelerate progress by offering subsidies and grants for sustainable housing projects.

- **Action Plan**:

○ Establish a National Green Housing Fund to support regional initiatives.

○ Provide low-interest loans for developers using sustainable methods.

c. Fostering Innovation Through Design Contests

Design contests can inspire groundbreaking ideas, mobilizing architects, engineers, and the private sector.

- **Action Plan**:

○ Organize national contests with themes like "Housing for Climate Resilience" or "Affordable Net-Zero Homes."

○ Partner with universities, NGOs, and the private sector to sponsor prizes and implement winning designs.

d. Public-Private Partnerships (PPPs)

Collaboration between government and private entities can drive innovation and efficiency.

- **Action Plan**:

○ Launch PPP programs to co-fund large-scale housing projects.

○ Private developers are required to include affordable housing units in major developments.

4. Engaging Stakeholders

To achieve these goals, it's essential to incentivize all stakeholders:

a. For Local Communities

- Offer subsidies to homeowners for retrofitting existing homes with sustainable features.
- Provide education and resources to encourage the adoption of green practices.

b. For Developers

- Provide financial incentives for meeting sustainability and affordability criteria.
- Reduce permitting times for projects that align with green housing standards.

c. For Innovators and Designers

- Sponsor grants for prototypes using cutting-edge materials and designs.
- Offer recognition and career opportunities for contest winners.

d. For Policymakers

- Align housing initiatives with broader climate and economic goals.
- Demonstrate the benefits of sustainable housing to voters and constituents.

5. Measuring Success

The effectiveness of these initiatives should be measured using clear metrics:

- **Environmental Impact**: Reduction in carbon emissions and energy use per household.
- **Affordability**: Decrease in the percentage of income spent on housing.
- **Economic Impact**: Job creation and local economic growth.
- **Scalability**: Number of replicable housing models developed.

Conclusion

Local, regional, and national goals must work in tandem to achieve sustainable, climate-proof housing for all. By leveraging local materials, empowering communities, and fostering innovation, it is possible to create a housing ecosystem that benefits both people and the planet. Governments can play a transformative role by offering incentives, revising policies, and championing creative solutions through initiatives like design contests.

The path forward is one of collaboration, creativity, and commitment. With sustained effort, sustainable housing can become the norm rather than the exception, bringing lasting benefits to individuals, communities, and nations.

Chapter 6

The Problem: Global Warming's Impact on Housing

The Problem: Global Warming's Impact on Housing

The most immediate and apparent challenge posed by global warming is the increasing intensity and frequency of extreme weather events. **Storms** are becoming more violent, **wildfires** are becoming more deadly, and **flooding** is becoming more widespread. In addition to the direct devastation caused by these events, there are cascading effects that impact housing and infrastructure.

Extreme Weather and Its Toll on Housing

In areas where natural disasters like hurricanes, wildfires, and flooding were once rare or seasonal, they are now becoming regular, sometimes annual occurrences. These events not only damage or destroy homes but also put lives at risk. Entire neighborhoods are wiped out in one storm. Wildfires burn down vast stretches of land, including entire communities, often before residents have a chance to evacuate. After the storms have passed, the long-term damage to homes often makes them uninhabitable for months or even years.

As **global warming** accelerates, the conditions that cause these extreme weather events are intensifying. For example, rising ocean temperatures and changing atmospheric conditions fuel stronger hurricanes and typhoons. Wildfires are more frequent and burn longer due to higher temperatures and prolonged droughts. In many areas, especially on the coast, homes that once stood proudly on solid ground are now at risk of being washed away or drowned by rising sea levels.

The Collapse of Infrastructure

Global warming is also taking a significant toll on **infrastructure**. Roads, bridges, power grids, and water systems that were built to withstand the climate of the past are now failing under the stresses of the present. And with each new climate disaster, the damage to infrastructure becomes more challenging and more expensive to repair.

Many cities around the world rely on outdated infrastructure that was designed with a different climate in mind. **Flooding** and **heatwaves** can cause power outages, disrupt transportation, and damage water supplies. The resulting breakdowns in the system not only make life difficult for residents but also drive up the costs of housing and living. In the face of these challenges, the task of maintaining and upgrading infrastructure becomes a massive burden for governments—one that they are often unprepared or unwilling to bear.

Financial Instability: The Collapse of the Insurance and Housing Markets

As housing becomes increasingly vulnerable to global warming, **insurance companies** are facing an existential crisis. More claims are being filed due to damage caused by natural disasters, and as the severity of these events increases, insurers are finding it harder to keep up. Some have already begun to pull out of high-risk areas, particularly those prone to flooding or wildfires. This leaves homeowners in a precarious situation, unable to insure their properties or, in many cases, unable to afford skyrocketing premiums.

At the same time, **banks** and financial institutions are becoming wary of lending in high-risk areas. They understand that homes built in flood zones or wildfire-prone areas may not survive the next disaster. As a result, homeowners are facing difficulties obtaining mortgages, and real estate markets in vulnerable regions are declining in value. This, in turn, creates a ripple effect: fewer people can afford homes, fewer houses are being built, and existing homes are left abandoned or unoccupied.

Coastal Areas Become Uninhabitable

One of the most troubling outcomes of global warming is the slow, relentless rise of sea levels. **Coastal areas that** were once thriving hubs of life and commerce are now increasingly at risk of submerging beneath the ocean. In some regions, the encroachment of the sea has already caused large-scale displacement, with residents having to abandon their homes and livelihoods. In the coming decades, millions of people living in coastal cities around the world may find themselves displaced due to rising sea levels, storm surges, and flooding.

This process of **coastal retreat** is already beginning in places like Miami, New York City, and Jakarta. As coastal areas become uninhabitable, the push to relocate puts additional strain on already overburdened cities. As more people flee to safer places, housing demand will skyrocket, further driving up prices and exacerbating the housing crisis.

The Solution: A Path Toward Resilience

It's easy to feel overwhelmed by the scale of the problem. Housing and infrastructure are not things that can be fixed with quick solutions. But there are steps we can take, both as individuals and as a society, to mitigate the effects of global warming on housing and ensure that people have homes that are safe, sustainable, and resilient to the changing climate.

Building Resilience into Housing Design

One of the most crucial steps in addressing the housing crisis caused by global warming is to **design buildings that can withstand extreme weather**. We must rethink how we build homes, focusing on durability, energy efficiency, and sustainability. This means constructing homes that are more **storm-resistant**, **fire-resistant**, and **energy-efficient**.

For example, houses built in hurricane-prone areas must withstand high winds and heavy rainfall. This can be achieved through **reinforced walls**, **wind-resistant roofing**, and the use of **storm shutters**. Similarly, homes in wildfire-prone areas should be built with **fire-resistant materials** and surrounded by **defensible space** to slow the spread of flames. In flood-prone areas, homes should be elevated above expected flood levels, with resilient drainage systems to handle heavy rain.

In addition to disaster-proofing homes, it's also important to design homes that are **energy-efficient**. As energy prices rise and the environmental impact of traditional power sources becomes more apparent, there is a growing need to reduce energy consumption. Homes that are well-insulated, equipped with solar panels, and designed to reduce heating and cooling costs will not only be more affordable to maintain but will also help reduce the overall demand for energy.

Upgrading Infrastructure to Meet New Realities

Governments must also invest in upgrading existing infrastructure to ensure it is resilient to the new realities of climate change. Roads, bridges, power grids, and water systems must be designed to withstand extreme weather conditions and be able to recover quickly from disruptions. In flood-prone areas, for example, cities should invest in **flood barriers**, **green infrastructure** (such as rain gardens and permeable pavement), and **early warning systems**.

The government must also take the lead in ensuring **adequate water and energy supply** during times of crisis. This could include investing in **renewable energy**, **desalination plants**, and **water storage systems** to ensure communities have access to essential resources, even in the face of natural disasters.

Creating Safe and Affordable Housing for All

One of the most pressing issues of the housing crisis is affordability. As extreme weather events continue to escalate, more people will be displaced from their homes, and housing demand will increase. Governments must create policies that ensure that **affordable housing** is available for those who need it most. This could involve **subsidizing rent**, providing **low-interest loans** for homebuyers, and incentivizing the construction of new, affordable homes in areas that are less vulnerable to climate change.

In addition to creating new housing, governments should invest in **retrofitting existing buildings** to make them more energy-efficient and disaster-resistant. Providing incentives for homeowners to upgrade their properties to meet modern climate standards can help reduce the long-term maintenance and repair costs.

Preparedness and Relocation Programs

In areas where climate change is already making living conditions untenable, **managed retreat** may be necessary. Governments should provide support for communities at risk of displacement due to sea-level rise or extreme weather events. This includes offering financial assistance for relocation and ensuring that displaced communities have access to safe, affordable housing in less vulnerable areas.

Conclusion: A Future of Resilience

The challenges posed by global warming are vast and complex, but they are not insurmountable. By investing in resilient housing, upgrading infrastructure, and ensuring that all people have access to safe, affordable homes, we can reduce the impact of climate change on our communities. The time to act is now. If we fail to prepare for the realities of global warming, we will only increase the risks of widespread housing destruction, financial instability, and human suffering.

Chapter 7

Building Resilience – Housing Solutions for a Changing Climate

The era of climate change demands a fundamental shift in how we design, build, and retrofit our homes. Our dwellings must evolve to withstand the growing threats posed by high winds, torrential rains, floods, and earthquakes while generating energy and food. This chapter explores strategies for designing resilient housing that can endure the forces of nature while remaining sustainable, adaptable, and, eventually, transportable to extreme environments like Mars, the Moon, or space.

Designing for High Winds: Tornadoes and Hurricanes

High winds, such as those generated by tornadoes and hurricanes, represent one of the most destructive forces homes face. Structures must be capable of withstanding wind speeds exceeding 200 mph while minimizing the dangers of flying debris.

Aerodynamic Design

Buildings in hurricane- and tornado-prone regions should incorporate aerodynamic designs to reduce wind resistance. Dome-shaped or hexagonal structures minimize flat surfaces that strong winds can easily damage. Roofs should be sloped and securely fastened to prevent uplift. Structural enhancements like hurricane straps, tie-downs, and reinforced roof trusses can increase wind resistance.

Reinforced Building Materials

Traditional wood-framed homes are vulnerable to high winds. Alternative materials such as reinforced concrete, steel framing, and fiber-reinforced composites offer greater durability. Innovations like **cross-laminated timber (CLT)**provide both strength and sustainability, combining renewable resources with advanced engineering.

Impact-Resistant Features

Impact-resistant windows, shutters, and roofing materials can prevent debris from penetrating the roof. Laminated glass, which incorporates a tough plastic interlayer, holds together even when shattered, while advanced composite shingles are designed to withstand extreme impacts.

Safe Rooms and Shelters

In tornado-prone regions, incorporating **storm-safe rooms** built to FEMA specifications can save lives. These shelters are typically constructed with steel-reinforced concrete and located within the home. Portable safe rooms, made of lightweight but robust materials, provide an option for retrofitting existing homes.

Strategies for High Water and Flooding

Flooding is a growing threat due to rising sea levels, heavier rainfall, and overflowing rivers. Flood-resistant homes require strategies to either elevate them above floodwaters or withstand prolonged water exposure.

Elevation and Stilts

In areas at high risk of flooding, elevating homes on stilts or pilings is a proven strategy. Houses are built above the base flood elevation (BFE), ensuring that living spaces remain safe even during severe floods. Modular designs with detachable foundations can be adapted for varying flood risks.

Waterproofing

Materials that resist water penetration, such as concrete with water-resistant admixtures, epoxy coatings, and advanced sealants, can prevent moisture damage. For retrofits, solutions include elevating electrical systems, sealing foundation cracks, and installing flood barriers.

Amphibious Design

An innovative approach to flooding is the **amphibious house**, which rests on a fixed foundation under normal conditions but floats during a flood. Such designs, already implemented in parts of the Netherlands, use buoyant foundations and guideposts to allow the structure to rise with water levels.

Passive Drainage and Retention Systems

Landscaping with porous surfaces, bioswales, and rain gardens can reduce water accumulation. Homes can also integrate passive drainage systems such as raised foundation vents and sump pumps to channel water away.

Earthquake Resilience

Earthquakes add another layer of complexity, requiring buildings to withstand ground motion and minimize collapse risk.

Base Isolation

Base isolation systems involve placing buildings on flexible bearings that absorb seismic energy. This technology decouples the structure from ground motion, reducing damage during an earthquake.

Flexible Structural Materials

Using materials like engineered wood, steel, and carbon-fiber reinforcements can improve flexibility, allowing structures to bend rather than break under stress. Walls and columns are designed to resist shear forces, while reinforced foundations anchor the building securely to the ground.

Seismic Dampers

Seismic dampers act as shock absorbers, converting kinetic energy from ground motion into heat or other forms of energy. Incorporating dampers into building frames helps maintain stability during earthquakes.

Lightweight Construction

For both new builds and retrofits, lightweight materials reduce the risk of structural failure. Roofs and upper stories are made lighter, and heavy components like brick facades are secured to prevent them from detaching during tremors.

Integrating Sustainability: Self-Sufficient Homes

Resilient housing must also address sustainability, reducing reliance on external resources for power, water, and even food. These homes are the precursors to self-contained units capable of functioning on Mars, the Moon, or in orbit.

Energy Generation and Storage

- **Solar Panels and Wind Turbines**: Roof-integrated solar panels and micro wind turbines generate renewable energy. Advances in **transparent solar cells** allow windows to double as energy sources.

- **Battery Storage Systems**: On-site battery systems, like those using lithium-ion or emerging solid-state technology, store energy for use during power outages or at night.

- **Geothermal Heating and Cooling**: Geothermal systems draw energy from the Earth's stable temperatures, reducing heating and cooling needs.

Water Collection and Recycling

- **Rainwater Harvesting**: Roofs can collect and channel rainwater into storage tanks for non-potable use. Advanced filtration systems make it suitable for drinking.

- **Greywater Systems**: Water from sinks, showers, and washing machines is recycled for irrigation and flushing toilets.

- **Desalination Units**: In coastal areas, compact desalination units can turn seawater into fresh water.

Food Production

- **Vertical Gardens**: Integrated into walls or rooftops, vertical gardens allow for year-round vegetable and herb cultivation.

- **Aquaponics and Hydroponics**: Closed-loop systems combine fish farming with plant growth, producing food without soil while recycling nutrients.
- **Smart Greenhouses**: Equipped with automated climate controls, these structures can optimize plant growth in limited spaces.

Modular and Adaptable Design: Toward Space Habitation

The ultimate evolution of resilient housing is the self-contained unit, designed not only for Earth's extreme environments but also for extraterrestrial conditions.

Transportable Housing Units

Modular homes built with lightweight, durable materials can be easily transported to disaster zones or deployed to Mars or the Moon. These units incorporate collapsible or expandable designs, allowing for efficient shipping and assembly.

Multi-Environment Resilience

- **Pressure-Sealed Construction**: On Mars or in orbit, homes must maintain internal pressure and regulate temperature. Using materials like aerogel insulation and graphene coatings ensures thermal stability.
- **Radiation Shielding**: Extraterrestrial habitats

incorporate layers of regolith (on Mars) or water to shield inhabitants from harmful radiation.

Self-Sustaining Ecosystems

Space habitats are closed-loop systems that recycle air, water, and waste. Earth-based prototypes use these principles, integrating bioreactors, water filtration, and waste composting to minimize external inputs.

Adaptable Architecture

Homes of the future will feature adaptable architecture, with movable walls, retractable roofs, and smart systems that respond to changing conditions. Robotics and artificial intelligence will manage resource use, monitor the structural health, and adjust environments in real-time.

Building for the Future

Combining resilience, sustainability, and adaptability, the housing solutions described in this chapter are not mere concepts but essential responses to a changing world. They demonstrate the power of human ingenuity to create homes that protect, sustain, and inspire. From standing firm against hurricanes to nurturing life on Mars, these designs represent a profound shift toward harmony with our environment—both on Earth and beyond.

. . .

In the face of this growing threat, the question is not whether we can afford to act but whether we can afford not to. The future of housing in a warming world depends on the choices we make today.

Chapter 8

Inclusive Housing Solutions – Bridging Gaps and Building Communities

Housing is not just about structures; it is about people. Yet, many individuals need access to stable housing due to personal limitations beyond their control. These challenges may stem from physical disabilities, mental health issues, lack of education, or systemic barriers that have entrenched inequality. This chapter explores a comprehensive approach to addressing housing inequities by empowering individuals with skills, designing systems for those unable to contribute, and fostering national unity toward sustainable, inclusive housing for all.

Part 1: Empowering People with Skills for Housing and Community Living

To ensure sustainable and affordable housing, we must equip individuals with the skills to own, operate, and manage their living spaces. Education and community-building programs can empower people to thrive in shared housing environments.

Teaching Essential Life Skills

For many, the path to successful independent or shared living begins with learning essential skills such as:

- **Financial Literacy**: Programs that teach budgeting, saving, and managing housing-related expenses like rent, utilities, and maintenance.

- **Home Maintenance**: Basic knowledge of repairs, cleaning, and upkeep, including plumbing, electrical work, and appliance care.

- **Conflict Resolution**: Training in effective communication and problem-solving to address disputes among housemates or neighbors.

- **Civic Engagement**: Understanding housing laws, tenant rights, and responsibilities fosters a sense of accountability and ownership.

These skills can be imparted through community centers, non-profits, and online platforms, ensuring accessibility for diverse populations.

Fostering Cooperation and Shared Living Skills

Living with others requires more than just cohabiting space; it demands collaboration, empathy, and the ability to share resources. Programs focused on communal living skills can teach individuals to:

- **Make Joint Decisions**: Training in consensus-building and democratic decision-making processes.
- **Share Resources**: Learning to efficiently share utilities, transportation, and common spaces.
- **Develop Community Bonds**: Activities that promote trust and friendship, such as group meals, shared projects, or cultural exchanges.

Case Studies: Successful Models

1 Cohousing Communities: These intentional neighborhoods combine private living spaces with shared facilities like kitchens and gardens. Residents collaborate on maintenance, decision-making, and community activities, fostering cooperation and reducing costs.

2 Housing First Initiatives: Programs like Finland's *Housing First* model provide individuals with stable housing first, followed by support services that help them acquire life skills and rebuild their lives.

By investing in education and community-building programs, we not only prepare individuals to manage their housing but also create environments where they can thrive together.

Part 2: Designing Inclusive Systems for Those Unable or Unwilling to Learn New Skills

Not everyone can acquire the skills necessary to manage their housing. This reality calls for innovative solutions that combine the strengths of those who can contribute with the needs of those who cannot, ensuring that everyone has access to stable and dignified housing.

Mixed-Ability Housing Models

Combining skilled and unskilled residents within a single community can create a balance where strengths are leveraged and weaknesses are supported. Key strategies include:

1 Collaborative Housing Structures:

o **Community Roles**: Residents with skills can take on specific responsibilities, such as managing finances, organizing events, or overseeing maintenance. Those unable to contribute can participate in smaller, manageable ways.

o **Shared Services**: On-site support services—like caretakers, social workers, or property managers—ensure that the needs of less independent residents are met.

2 Incentivized Support Networks:

o **Compensation Models**: Skilled residents who assist others (e.g., teaching, caretaking, or mentoring) can receive reduced rent or other benefits.

o **Co-living Contracts**: Agreements outline

expectations, contributions, and support mechanisms, fostering mutual accountability.

Dedicated Housing for the Most Vulnerable

For individuals who cannot participate in communal living, specialized housing options are essential:

- **Assisted Living Facilities**: Homes designed for individuals with disabilities or chronic health issues, staffed with trained professionals.

- **Permanent Supportive Housing**: Long-term housing integrated with healthcare, mental health services, and substance abuse treatment for vulnerable populations.

- **Tiny Home Villages**: Low-cost, small-scale housing units that provide privacy while being part of a supportive community.

Technology-Enabled Solutions

Advances in technology can bridge gaps between residents with varying abilities:

- **Smart Homes**: Equipped with automation for lighting, heating, and appliances, reducing the burden of daily tasks.

- **Remote Support Services**: Virtual check-ins and online resources for health, education, and conflict resolution.

- **Shared Economy Platforms**: Apps that facilitate

resource sharing and community-building within housing complexes.

By creating environments where skilled and unskilled residents can coexist and complement one another, we foster a sense of interdependence and inclusivity that strengthens communities.

Part 3: Unifying the Nation Around Housing Equity and Sustainability

The challenge of providing equitable, sustainable housing is a national issue that requires collective action. Achieving this goal involves uniting people across socioeconomic and political divides and motivating them through shared incentives and benefits.

Incentivizing Participation

Motivating individuals, businesses, and communities to invest in inclusive housing can be achieved through:

1 Financial Incentives:

o **Tax Credits**: Offering tax breaks to developers and landlords who prioritize affordable, sustainable housing.

o **Grants and Subsidies**: Providing funding for retrofitting homes, building energy-efficient structures, or creating mixed-income communities.

2 Access to Public Resources:

○ **Priority Access**: Rewarding participation in housing programs with enhanced access to public transit, parks, and community centers.

○ **Workforce Development Opportunities**: The goal is to connect housing program participants with job training and employment opportunities.

3 Social Recognition:

○ **Awards and Certification**: Recognizing businesses and individuals who contribute to inclusive housing efforts.

○ **Public Campaigns**: Highlighting success stories to inspire others to join the movement.

Building a National Consensus

Uniting the country requires a shared vision of what housing equity and sustainability can achieve. This can be accomplished through:

1 Public Awareness Campaigns:

○ Media initiatives that emphasize the societal benefits of inclusive housing, such as reduced homelessness, improved mental health, and stronger communities.

○ Educational programs in schools and colleges to instill the values of empathy, cooperation, and sustainability.

2 Policy and Legislation:

○ Enacting housing policies that prioritize mixed-income and mixed-ability developments.

○ Creating regulations that encourage sustainable building practices and retrofitting.

3 Grassroots Movements:

○ Empowering local communities to advocate for housing solutions tailored to their unique needs.

○ Establishing neighborhood committees to oversee the implementation and success of housing programs.

Collaborative Efforts

Real progress will require partnerships between governments, non-profits, private developers, and residents. Examples include:

- **Public-Private Partnerships**: Joint ventures to fund and develop affordable housing projects.
- **Community Land Trusts**: Non-profit organizations that manage land for affordable housing, ensuring long-term access for low-income residents.

The Role of Shared Values

Ultimately, a unified approach to housing requires embracing shared values of equity, sustainability, and mutual responsibility. By fostering a culture of care and cooperation, we can transform housing from a commodity into a fundamental human right.

A Path Toward Inclusive Housing for All

By empowering individuals with the skills to manage their housing, creating systems for those who cannot, and uniting the nation around a shared vision, we can address the housing crisis in a way that benefits everyone. This chapter highlights the possibility of inclusive housing and its necessity in building a society where everyone has a place to call home.

Chapter 9

Sustainable Urban Infrastructure – Building Cities for People, Not Cars

As urban populations grow, the need for sustainable infrastructure that prioritizes transit-oriented development (TOD), pedestrian-friendly spaces, and environmentally conscious construction has never been more urgent. The goal is to redesign cities to make walking, cycling, and person-powered transport the fastest, easiest, and most sustainable methods for moving people and goods. This chapter explores how cities can achieve this transformation by aligning development around transit, adopting net-zero materials and practices, and unifying communities and governments to embrace a car-free future.

Transit-Oriented Development: Redesigning Cities Around People

The Core of Transit-Oriented Development (TOD)

TOD places housing, businesses, and amenities within walking or cycling distance of high-quality public transportation. This approach reduces car dependency, promotes community engagement, and fosters sustainable urban growth.

Key Principles of TOD:

1 **Proximity to Transit**: Developments are clustered within a five to ten-minute walk from transit hubs.

2 **Mixed-Use Design**: Residential, commercial, and recreational spaces are integrated to create vibrant, walkable neighborhoods.

3 **Density**: Compact urban planning maximizes land use and reduces urban sprawl.

4 **Public Spaces**: Parks, plazas, and pedestrian zones enhance community life and encourage non-motorized transport.

Strategies for Implementing TOD

1 **Zoning Reforms**: Local governments must adopt zoning laws that prioritize mixed-use, high-density developments near transit hubs.

2 **Public-Private Partnerships**: Collaborations with developers can ensure affordable housing and sustainable building practices in TOD projects.

3 **Universal Design**: Infrastructure should be accessible to all, including people with disabilities, parents with strollers, and older people.

Case Studies

- **Copenhagen, Denmark**: Known for its bike-friendly infrastructure, Copenhagen integrates cycling lanes with public transit and ensures that all city areas are accessible by bike or foot.

- **Portland, Oregon**: The city's urban growth boundary and light rail system have successfully reduced car dependency while encouraging TOD.

Prioritizing Person-Powered Transport

Infrastructure for Walking and Cycling

To make walking and cycling the preferred modes of transportation, cities must create safe, convenient, and attractive infrastructure.

Key Components of Pedestrian and Bicycle Infrastructure:

1 **Dedicated Bike Lanes**: Protected lanes separated from motor traffic ensure safety for cyclists.

2 **Widened Sidewalks**: Spacious, well-maintained sidewalks promote pedestrian use.

3 **Crosswalk Safety**: Raised crosswalks, traffic-calming measures, and extended walk signals prioritize pedestrian movement.

4 **End-of-Trip Facilities**: Secure bike parking,

showers, and changing facilities make cycling viable for daily commutes.

Bicycle-Friendly Policies

1 **Bike-Share Programs**: Affordable and accessible bike-sharing systems encourage cycling, especially for short trips.

2 **Subsidies for Bikes**: Governments can offer rebates or tax credits for purchasing bicycles or e-bikes.

3 **Car-Free Zones**: Designating downtown areas as pedestrian-only creates incentives to walk or bike.

Innovative Person-Powered Transport

Emerging technologies and ideas are expanding the possibilities for sustainable transport:

- **Cargo Bikes**: Designed for carrying goods, these bikes can replace delivery vehicles for short-distance logistics.
- **Walking Pods**: Small, electric-assisted pods for people with mobility challenges offer sustainable alternatives to cars.

Sustainable Materials and Construction Practices

Materials for Roads, Bridges, and Buildings

Urban infrastructure must prioritize materials and

methods that minimize environmental impact while maximizing durability and sustainability.

Sustainable Materials:

1 **Recycled Materials**: Asphalt made from recycled plastics, steel, or rubber reduces waste.

2 **Green Concrete**: By incorporating carbon-sequestering technologies, green concrete reduces CO_2 emissions during production.

3 **Bamboo and Cross-Laminated Timber (CLT)**: Renewable and strong, these materials are ideal for sustainable building construction.

Innovative Designs:

- **Permeable Pavements**: These pavements allow water to filter through, reducing runoff and recharging groundwater.

- **Modular Construction**: Prefabricated modules minimize waste and speed up construction while using eco-friendly materials.

- **Living Infrastructure**: Green roofs, vertical gardens, and bio-walls integrate plants into urban design, improving air quality and reducing heat islands.

Net-Zero Construction Practices

1 **Energy-Efficient Designs**: Solar panels, passive heating, and cooling systems reduce energy demand in buildings.

2 Circular Construction: Reusing materials from deconstructed buildings reduces waste and resource extraction.

3 On-Site Renewable Energy: Wind, solar, and geothermal energy integrated into construction projects ensure long-term sustainability.

Motivating the Shift Away from Cars

Despite the benefits of walking, cycling, and transit-oriented development, many people remain attached to car-dependent lifestyles. Transforming urban mobility requires addressing cultural and practical barriers. Many do not have a choice and must use a car to get to work, school, and recreational activities.

Incentives for Adopting Sustainable Transport

1 Financial Rewards:

- **Tax Breaks**: Offering deductions for using public transit, cycling, or purchasing sustainable transport solutions like e-bikes.

- **Congestion Pricing**: Charging fees for driving in dense urban areas discourages car use while funding public transportation.

2 Access Benefits:

- **Priority Parking**: Reserved spaces for carpoolers or cyclists near transit hubs.

○ **Faster Commutes**: Dedicated bus lanes and cycle highways can make sustainable travel quicker than driving.

3 Subsidized Public Transit: Lower fares, free passes, or employer-sponsored transit programs make public transportation more appealing.

Cultural Campaigns

1 Public Awareness: Highlight the environmental, health, and economic benefits of walking, cycling, and public transport through media campaigns.

2 Education Programs: Schools and community groups can teach the benefits of sustainable transport from an early age.

3 Showcasing Success: Sharing stories of cities and individuals who have successfully transitioned to car-free lifestyles inspires others to follow.

Addressing Practical Barriers

1 Improved Transit: Reliable, frequent, and comfortable public transportation systems reduce the need for cars.

2 Multi-Modal Integration: Seamlessly connecting walking, cycling, and transit with shared mobility options like scooters or ride-shares makes travel flexible.

3 Urban Design: Compact city layouts with mixed-use neighborhoods reduce travel distances, making walking and cycling more viable.

Government and Community Unification

Transforming urban infrastructure requires a united effort from governments, businesses, and communities. A coordinated approach ensures equitable, sustainable, and efficient progress.

Government Leadership

1 Policy and Legislation: Mandating TOD, sustainable materials, and car-free zones through robust urban planning policies.

2 Funding and Subsidies: Providing grants for sustainable construction projects, bike-share programs, and public transit expansions.

3 Monitoring and Enforcement: Ensuring compliance with sustainability goals through regular audits and penalties for violations.

Community Engagement

1 Public Consultations: Involving residents in the planning process ensures solutions meet community needs.

2 Pilot Projects: Small-scale trials of car-free zones, bike lanes, or TOD initiatives allow communities to experience benefits firsthand.

3 Local Champions: Empowering community leaders to advocate for sustainable changes builds grassroots support.

Collaborative Partnerships

1 Private Sector Involvement: Encouraging businesses to invest in sustainable urban infrastructure through tax incentives or recognition programs can advance sustainable development.

2 Non-Profit Organizations: Partnering with environmental groups to educate and mobilize citizens.

3 Global Networks: Learning from successful international models like Singapore's public transit or Amsterdam's cycling culture.

National Vision and Goals

1 Unified Messaging: Framing sustainable urban infrastructure as a national priority for economic growth, public health, and environmental protection.

2 Civic Pride: Encouraging cities to compete for recognition as leaders in sustainability fosters innovation and progress.

A Blueprint for the Future

Sustainable urban infrastructure is not just about reducing environmental impact; it's about creating cities where people can thrive. By prioritizing transit-oriented development, designing for walking and cycling, adopting sustainable materials, and motivating communities to embrace change, we can build cities that are not only functional but also equitable, healthy, and inspiring. This chapter lays the foundation for a collective journey toward urban environments that prioritize people over cars, setting a precedent for sustainable living worldwide.

Chapter 10

Transitioning from Evictions to Housing Solutions: A Government-Led Initiative

Housing is a basic human need, yet the current system often fails to provide stability for tenants and landlords alike. Today, governments primarily intervene in housing through the eviction process, stepping in when tenants cannot pay rent, fail to maintain the rental unit or disrupt the peace of a building. This reactive approach leaves countless individuals without homes while perpetuating adversarial relationships between tenants and landlords. To address this systemic failure, governments must transition from enforcing evictions to proactively ensuring housing for all. This chapter outlines a framework for how such a transition could occur, focusing on the roles and responsibilities of tenants and landlords, government oversight, and conflict resolution mechanisms.

The Framework for Transition

The government's new role would center on organizing entities to ensure that everyone has access to housing. This requires shifting from punitive measures, such as evictions, to proactive measures, such as creating and maintaining an adequate housing stock. Under this system, housing would no longer be seen solely as a private market commodity but as a shared societal responsibility.

To make this transition, the government would adopt a dual accountability model where both landlords and tenants are held responsible for fulfilling their roles. Landlords would remain responsible for providing safe, habitable units that meet agreed-upon standards. Tenants, in turn, would be required to pay a monthly fee to cover the building's expenses, maintain their apartments, avoid causing damage, and take measures to prevent pest problems. Both parties would be licensed by the government, ensuring they understand and can fulfill their responsibilities.

Qualifying for Housing

To qualify for housing under this system, tenants would need to meet certain criteria and complete a government-mandated course. This course would cover:

• The basics of maintaining an apartment (e.g., cleanliness, pest control, and basic repairs).

- Understanding lease agreements and their obligations.

- How to report maintenance issues or disputes responsibly.

Upon completing the course, tenants would receive a rental license, certifying them as eligible to rent a government-approved housing unit. Landlords would also need to obtain a permit, demonstrating that they have met all property legal and safety standards. These certifications create a baseline of accountability and ensure that both parties enter the agreement with a shared understanding of their roles.

Roles and Responsibilities of Landlords

Landlords would be responsible for ensuring their properties are safe, habitable, and well-maintained. Specific obligations would include:

1 **Providing Safe Housing**: Ensuring that units comply with building codes and safety regulations.

2 **Maintenance and Repairs**: Addressing structural issues, plumbing, heating, and other essential services promptly.

3 **Transparency in Lease Agreements**: Clearly outline the terms of the rental agreement, including rules for shared spaces and tenant responsibilities.

4 **Engagement with Tenants**: Communicating proactively to address tenant concerns and fostering a collaborative relationship.

Failure to meet these responsibilities would trigger government intervention. For example, if a landlord neglects repairs or violates safety standards, the government could impose penalties or temporarily assign a third-party manager to oversee the property.

Roles and Responsibilities of Tenants

Tenants would be expected to:

1 **Pay the Monthly Fee**: Cover the cost of building expenses as outlined in their lease agreements.

2 **Maintain the Apartment**: Keep the unit clean, avoid causing damage, and ensure it remains pest-free.

3 **Respect Building Policies**: Adhere to community rules and avoid disruptive behaviors that affect neighbors.

4 **Report Issues Promptly**: Notify landlords or property managers of maintenance needs or other concerns in a timely manner.

If tenants fail to meet these responsibilities, the government could intervene by requiring additional training or, in severe cases, relocating the tenant to a more supervised housing arrangement.

Conflict Resolution Mechanisms

Conflicts between landlords and tenants are inevitable, but the new system would prioritize mediation over punitive measures. Government-trained housing mediators would be available to resolve disputes, such as disagreements over maintenance responsibilities or accusations of rule violations. The mediation process would:

1 Facilitate open dialogue between landlords and tenants.

2 Provide clear, actionable resolutions to disputes.

3 Document outcomes to ensure accountability.

If mediation fails, the government could step in to enforce solutions, such as mandating repairs or issuing penalties for rule violations.

Licensing and Training Requirements

Both landlords and tenants would need to obtain licenses to participate in the housing system. For landlords, this would involve:

- Passing property inspections to ensure compliance with safety and habitability standards.

- Completing a course on property management, tenant relations, and conflict resolution.

For tenants, the licensing process would focus on:

- Educating them about their rights and responsibilities.

- Ensuring they understand how to maintain their housing and fulfill their obligations under the lease.

These licensing programs would establish a baseline of knowledge and accountability, reducing misunderstandings and conflicts while fostering a culture of shared responsibility.

Transitioning from Evictions to Housing Solutions

Under the current system, eviction is often the default response to tenant noncompliance. In the proposed model, eviction would be replaced by structured interventions. For instance:

1 **Early Intervention Programs**: When a tenant falls behind on payments, the government could provide temporary financial assistance or connect them with job training programs to improve their ability to pay rent.

2 **Support for Landlords**: If a landlord faces significant financial losses due to tenant noncompliance, the government could offer subsidies or grants to cover expenses, ensuring the property remains viable.

3 **Relocation Assistance**: In extreme cases where a tenant cannot meet their obligations despite support, the government would arrange for alternative housing, ensuring the tenant is not left homeless.

These measures shift the focus from punishment to problem-solving, ensuring that housing remains a stable and accessible resource.

Building Collaborative Relationships

Landlords and tenants could interact in ways that foster collaboration and mutual respect. Examples include:

- **Tenant Committees**: Allowing tenants to participate in building management decisions fosters a sense of ownership and community.

- **Regular Check-Ins**: Establish routine meetings between landlords and tenants to discuss maintenance, address concerns, and build trust.

- **Incentive Programs**: Rewarding tenants and landlords for maintaining their responsibilities, such as discounts for timely rent payments or tax breaks for well-managed properties.

These interactions create more stable and harmonious living environments by encouraging cooperation rather than conflict.

The Government's Role in Ensuring Compliance

The government would act as the ultimate arbiter, ensuring that both landlords and tenants fulfill their obligations. This oversight would include:

- **Routine Inspections**: Conducting regular checks to ensure that properties meet safety and habitability standards.

- **Complaint Resolution**: Investigating and resolving complaints from tenants or landlords about noncompliance.

- **Enforcement Mechanisms**: Imposing penalties, such as fines or temporary license suspensions, for violations by landlords or tenants.

In severe cases, the government could take more direct action, such as assigning third-party management to a poorly maintained property or relocating a disruptive tenant to a more suitable housing arrangement.

Creating a System of Accountability and Support

The transition from evictions to a government-organized housing system represents a significant shift in how society addresses housing needs. By establishing clear roles and responsibilities for landlords and tenants, implementing robust training and licensing programs, and providing effective conflict resolution mechanisms, this model creates a foundation for stable and equitable housing. The government's proactive involvement ensures that housing is treated not as a privilege but as a fundamental right, fostering a society where everyone has the opportunity to thrive.

Chapter 11

Building a Sustainable Housing Future

The eviction process is a lose-lose situation for both landlords and tenants. Landlords face significant financial losses when tenants are unable to pay rent. The eviction process can take months, during which landlords forgo rental income and may incur additional costs to repair damages caused by departing tenants. In some cases, tenants under threat of eviction engage in nuisance activities, further complicating matters for the property owners. On the other hand, tenants experience profound disruptions to their lives. Evictions force families out of their homes, often leaving them with little to no money for alternative housing. They face the daunting challenge of finding a new place to live, frequently while dealing with damaged credit or lack of references, which exacerbates their financial and emotional stress.

For communities, the broader implications of evictions ripple outward. Neighborhoods may suffer from increased instability as evictions disrupt social cohesion and local economies. Children in evicted families often face interruptions in education, and health problems can arise from stress and inadequate living conditions. This vicious cycle underscores the urgent need for interventions that prevent evictions and create pathways to sustainable housing for all.

Why Government Action is Essential

The government must step in to address homelessness and the housing crisis because stable housing is foundational to a functioning society. With secure housing, individuals can maintain employment, care for their families, and contribute productively to the economy. Homelessness places enormous strain on public resources, including emergency healthcare services, law enforcement, and social welfare programs. By investing in housing solutions, governments can reduce these costs while improving the quality of life for millions of people.

Furthermore, the housing crisis intersects with the broader challenge of preparing the country for the impacts of global warming. Aging and inadequate housing infrastructure must withstand the increasing frequency of extreme weather events. Strengthening and modernizing the built environment—including retrofitting existing structures and ensuring new developments are resilient—is essential for safeguarding communities against the evolving threats of climate change.

Education and training are also critical components of the solution. By incorporating housing education into K-12 curricula and expanding colleges and vocational school programs, the government can prepare the next generation to own, operate, and maintain housing sustainably. This educational investment would empower individuals with the skills to manage properties effectively, reduce maintenance costs, and create resilient, energy-efficient housing that benefits individuals and communities.

Sustaining Affordable Housing in the Built Environment

The built environment plays a pivotal role in ensuring access to affordable housing. Governments must prioritize policies that incentivize the development of housing that is both affordable and sustainable. This includes offering tax breaks or subsidies to developers who build energy-efficient, low-cost housing and implementing zoning reforms to allow for more diverse housing options. Mixed-use developments, for example, can combine residential, commercial, and public spaces in ways that promote affordability and reduce the need for long commutes.

Additionally, existing buildings must not be overlooked. Retrofitting older structures to improve energy efficiency and resilience to climate impacts can extend their lifespan and make them more affordable to operate. Such retrofits include installing solar panels, upgrading insulation, and transitioning to renewable energy sources. These improvements reduce utility costs for tenants and decrease the environmental impact of housing, aligning with broader sustainability goals.

Uniting People and Resources for a Shared Goal

Addressing the housing crisis requires a united effort from all sectors of society. Governments must foster collaboration between landlords, tenants, builders, and community organizations to create solutions that work for everyone. By establishing partnerships and open lines of communication, stakeholders can identify shared goals, such as reducing evictions and increasing the availability of affordable housing. Public campaigns to raise awareness about housing issues and the benefits of collaborative approaches can also help build consensus and momentum for change.

Education and training will remain central to these efforts. Expanding vocational programs and apprenticeships in construction, property management, and renewable energy installation can create a skilled workforce dedicated to building and maintaining affordable, sustainable housing. Schools and community colleges should integrate these topics into their curricula, ensuring that young people understand the importance of sustainable housing and are equipped with the skills to contribute to its development.

Defining and enforcing building standards is another critical step. These standards should prioritize resilience to climate change, energy efficiency, and affordability. By establishing clear benchmarks for new construction and retrofits, governments can ensure that housing stock is prepared to withstand future challenges while meeting the needs of current residents. Furthermore, these standards should be developed within the context of modern urban planning principles, such as creating walkable, auto-free cities that reduce emissions and promote community well-being.

A Vision for the Future

Imagine a city where housing is affordable, sustainable, and integrated into a vibrant, auto-free urban environment. Streets are lined with energy-efficient buildings powered by renewable energy, and public spaces are designed for community interaction and resilience against extreme weather events. In this vision, housing is not just a place to live but a cornerstone of a thriving, equitable society.

To achieve this future, governments must unite people, resources, and expertise around a shared vision. They must invest in education, enforce sustainable building standards, and support the development of innovative housing models that prioritize community and environmental well-being.

Taking decisive action now can transform the housing crisis into an opportunity to build a stronger, more sustainable future for everyone.

This book has outlined the challenges and opportunities of addressing the housing crisis. The final chapter underscores the urgency of the moment and the necessity of a coordinated, forward-thinking approach. Together, we can create a world where everyone has access to safe, affordable, and sustainable housing—a foundation for a brighter, more resilient future.

About the Author

Dan Paul grew up fishing, playing sports, and building houses in Lake Wobegon. After attending the University of Wisconsin, Madison, and working at the linear fusion reactor lab, he explored alternatives to the dominant codes. While staying in coops, communes, and squats around the country, he learned the fundamentals of setting up and operating progressive, radical, and sustainable alternatives to the codes of the corporations and nation. Making affordable and sustainable housing for the last 4 decades has provided a reason for this book. Living without a vehicle for that period has given me an appreciation for transit oriented development, auto free zones and auto free cities.

Also by Dan Paul

Philosophy of Action Design and Multiplicity by Dan Paul

Book 1 Auto Free Design

Book 2 Workers Health Handbook

Book 3 Save Your Life Prevent Hospital Use

Book 4 Coop Owners Handbook

Book 5 Eye on AI Meeting Needs Sustainably

Book 6 Travels on the Nomadic Terrain

Book 7 Tales of the Urban Shaman

Book 8 Housing in the Danger Zone

Book 9 Corona Time

Book 10 Philosophy of Design, Action and Multiplicity

Coming soon

Auto Free USA

Websites

https://viaradmedia.org

https://autofreedesign.com

http://workershealthhandbook.com

http://sylphu.com

Social Media

https://www.facebook.com/profile.php?id=61555599616489

https://twitter.com/jonblu

https://www.instagram.com/jonblu61/

Made in the USA
Monee, IL
09 November 2026

67380376R00066